SIMPLE DAY TRADING STRATEGIES

A Beginners Guide into the World of Day Trading Strategies

Bradley Thornton

Legal notice

Table of Contents

Chapter 1

INTRODUCTION TO SIMPLE DAY TRADING STOCK STRATEGIES.DEFINITION OF IMPORTANT TERMS.

Simple Day Trading -refers to market positions which are held only a short time; typically, the trader opens and closes a position the same day, but positions can be held for a period as well. The position can be either long (buying outright) or short ("borrowing" shares, then offering to sell at a certain price). A day trader is looking to take advantage of volatility during the trading day, and reduce "overnight risk" caused by events (such as a bad earnings surprise) that might happen after the markets are closed.

Trading strategy -is a fixed plan that is designed to achieve a profitable return by going long or short in markets. The main reasons that a properly researched trading strategy helps are its verifiability, quantifiably, consistency, and objectivity.

Entry Point - The price at which an investor buys an investment. The entry point is usually a component of a predetermined trading strategy for minimizing investment risk and removing the emotion from trading decisions. Recognizing a good entry point is the first step in achieving a successful trade.

Swing Trading- Is a short-term trading method that can be used when trading stocks and options. Whereas Day Trading positions last less than one day, Swing Trading positions typically last two to six days, but may last as long as two weeks.

The concept got a bad reputation in the 1990's when many beginners began to day trade, jumping onto the new online trading platforms without applying tested stock trading strategies. They thought they could "go to work" in their pajamas and make a fortune in stock trades with very little knowledge or effort. This proved not to be the case.

Day trading is not all that complicated once you learn a simple, rules-based strategy for anticipating market moves, such as that taught at Online Trading Academy.

Lots of stock traders will explain that the stock trading technique is very often said to be exactly like a stock trading system that is designed to be used and traded in the stock market. However, a stock trading strategy does involve a complete system which includes not only entry and exit rules but the stock selection, risk control and cash management. For the specialized stock trader, the specialized approach to a stock trading technique is centered mainly in price action. The "bottom-up" stock trading strategy is the most popular fundamental method employed by analysts. You should always keep in mind that a great stock trading strategy is both simple and practical. Once the set of rules and guidelines that make the overall stock trading strategy happen to be identified and implemented by a stock trader, the trader must remember to remain open-minded so that the trading strategy could be fine-tuned and adjusted to new conditions in the stock market.

When trading stocks using technical evaluation, your trading plan will specify the conditions and requirements for getting into and exiting trades. A great stock trading strategy will specify the optimum quantity of shares to trade in a given period. Money management is at the heart of a great stock trading strategy. Stock traders who use a good strong stock trading strategy know and understand that money control may be the total answer to continued growth in their trading account. Because of this, the money management component of a stock trading system has often been known as "the golden rule to stock trading."

Regardless of what stock trading strategies you employ and trade make sure to: remain unemotional and never invest money you need for rental, the home loan, bills, or even food. By examining your routines and actions, you can significantly enhance your stock trading strategy. Poor stock trading strategy actions are often caused by uncontrolled emotional reactions, while some are just simply the consequence of poor stock trading routines. Your trading objective is to make your stock trading technique organized, logical and persistent at all times. By studying and searching closely at market conditions to look for the present trend for the market, a successful trader is then able to make the best stock trading strategy to be used for the next day. Armed with this market information and his trading plan in hand, the trader is less likely to be influenced by uncontrolled emotions. When you are conscious of your trading, and by constantly trying to improve your stock trading strategy, you will soon develop and discover the set of actions that will make trading success a practice for you.

Stock screening is a fundamental stock trading strategy and tool which involves the trader screening the entire world of securities for possibly advantageous stocks for trading. A few traders prefer to use moving averages in their stock screening. For instance, the trader may be searching for stocks which are in an uptrend and are over their two hundred days and 50-day moving averages. The use of moving averages in a trading strategy is quite simple, and this technique is best suited to markets and stocks which pattern well.

While other stock traders search for stocks which are ready to breakout from a pullback.

A word about Market Balance comes after. It is said to be obtained when the market price of stock or security represents the typical intrinsic estimates of all traders and investors. Market Efficiency means that the more efficient the market is the greater the degree that security price reflects all the information offered which may influence the price of the stock or security.

If your stock trading technique is not fitted to short-term market conditions; you need to adjust your strategy quickly, and if required, don't trade. Short term trading combined with long term stock investing needs to be part of your trading plan if you want to build money while trading stocks.

A great way for an individual to make money is through stock trading. Stock trading can have a large annual return for those wishing to save for large items, vacations, renovations, retirement funds or for an alternate way to grow your money. Although the unpredictability makes people cautious, the return is often greater than leaving the money in a savings account of bond certificates.

Luckily, there are some basic stock trading tips available for individuals wanting to make progress in the stock market, mainly, in setting up the registration of an account and developing market strategies related to your investments which ultimately helps you make money on the stock market.

The most important step is the registration of an account with an online broker, there are brokers who are inexpensive and will help you set up an account immediately. An initial investment of five hundred dollars or more is often required upon registration of the account. Also, the broker will charge a minimal commission fee to facilitate the transactions for you. Once the account is set up, trading can begin immediately.

For those who are not technically savvy or who prefer less personal interaction in dealing with their investment account, full-service online brokers can manage the account as well. A higher an initial investment will be required to set up the account as well as a superior commission fee; however, the broker can offer investment advice about your portfolio in conjunction with your account. This offers many individuals a professional opinion about their investment possibilities.

The most important of stock trading basics to undertake once you've established a stock trading account is to do your homework and research your investments carefully. Stock market trading is often driven by the news and financial conditions surrounding a company and industry, and knowing these conditions can help you make a more informed investment decision.

There are stock trading systems which allow an individual to see the information and news regarding a company in real time thus permitting the novice investor to acquire additional knowledge and the experienced investor an opportunity on the market. News and related information can be found through websites of major financial news service organizations or internet portal as well as the company's website.

A third of successful trading is based on the understanding of the risks f the market. There is a possibility of losing money as well as gaining a great deal but there are also tax implications, and an investor must be aware and prepared for these situations. Knowing the details can help alleviate the stress of some trading decisions and allow you greater confidence in pursuing your venture.

There are many brokerage websites, financial information sites and new investor forums that also offer stock trading basics. There is a vast amount of information available to the independent investor to feel confident entering the market and the knowledge to expand on the investments, whether present or future, to achieve what you want.

The day trade involves the practice of trading financial products like stocks, options shares, futures, and currency. The transaction during the day ends the same day before the markets close.

Day trade can help make you high profits. We know people have succeeded in the day, and some even claim million dollar profits in a year.

However, the day trade, like other types of transactions on the market, comes with its risks. The fact remains - each day can make some money, but we must also remember that the day can also make you suffer serious financial losses.

The day trading is considered a very risky type of operation. We know that many people do go bankrupt because of the day trade.

Day Exchange is recommended for people at the same time, experience, and adequate funding. You must realize that almost every trader suffers losses during the first month of the practice of the day. Many of them didn't wait to recover their loss; they just gave up trading completely.

So keep in mind that every great player must have suffered a few losses when they started out

If you want to do day trading, you can minimize the risks and increase the opportunity to be able to enjoy it. To be a better trader try ans work with some of the following suggested strategies:

Six kinds of strategies are used for day traders make a profit:

Trends Following

Traders use this strategy of buying stocks on the rise or short-sell if it is declining. It is based on the idea that the trend will continue.

Range Trading

Traders use the strategy of buying stocks at low prices and selling when they rise. It is assumed that once a stock peaks, it will start going down and will do so for a while.

News Strategy

Trading with a news strategy is the most basic and common approach. Traders buy a stock that was in the news as rising, and they see following bad news.

Scalping

This is the strategy where traders liquidated and established a good position quickly. This normally happens in a matter of seconds or minutes.

Short Stocks Strategy

This strategy assumes that a purchased stock is about to rise. Another strategy of shorting stocks is that traders borrow stocks from market brokers and sand resell in the hope that prices will come down and then buy again.

Day trading is a complex issue. You need some of these qualities to succeed at it:

First, it is a mentally challenging operation. You need to be able to keep your focus for long periods of time.

And then you need to be good with your money. Do not go overboard in the hope of making your millions quickly.

Do not expect to start making money immediately. You will probably lose out in the first month. That's why you need to have a good amount of money to last you through this time.

Persons, who are thinking of making investments must invest in shares, offered that they realize the trading process, and are aware of trading shares hints and Stock market techniques which can be used to boost the possibility of generating winning stock trading decisions. Here are a lot of tips of trading that are worth applying:

Method #1: Discover everything you could regard the business shares you're interested in.

One of the several most basic techniques for stock traders is this: acquire enough data related to the specific shares which have caught your interest; the reputation of the organization selling the shares; the monetary data regarding that company, and so on. If you have no idea related to the firm offering the stocks, you ought to not invest in shares, because in case you do, you're investing blindly, and which can make you lose capital.

Method #2: Before opening an online account, exploration on the online stock marketing firm/company first.

Included in the list of essential investing stocks secrets is for you to analysis on the reviews and comments regarding the Internet stock-marketing business before you open an account with them. It is a need to that you sign up with a company that has a great reputation. Working with a well-reputed firm is surely the component of Stock market strategies because if the business you create an account with is not quite an expert on stock-trading, or does not have complete resources about the market, you can't expect to earnings from stocks.

Way #3: Always are logical once generating decisions.

One of the most beneficial tricks of trading that have to be utilized by people who invest in stocks is to always make decisions dependent on their logic, or their brains. In any investing e. g. Stock investing, currency investing, etc., an element of vital investing stocks tricks is to avoid investing depending on the emotions or feelings you have; instead trade just with a clear head/mind. Never engaging in emotional trading, is listed in the first Stock market secrets that every single trader ought to make utilize of.

Generating share investments will be able to lead you to the path of richness, obviously, when you follow the secrets and tricks shared in this article. You need to not invest in shares according to wild guesses, and if you are clueless about the processes, trends, and secrets involved in the market. Remember that aside from knowing the steps on producing share trades, you also should fully understand trading shares strategies and incorporate them whenever you trade in the Stock-market.

If you are an experienced trader or investor, then you have probably used options trading rolling strategies. To put it simply it is a strategy where you would move your strike point to a new strike point within the same month as your original transaction. The term rolling essentially means moving.

In options trading, the movement happens when you move from one strike price or point to another strike price or point. This can be accomplished when you move points vertically or horizontally. Moving points vertically means you will be making this transaction within the same month as your original strike point. Moving points horizontally means you will request that this transaction takes place within a different month from your original transaction.

Traders and investors understand that for them to maximize their returns they need to use the covered call strategy each month consecutively over a long period. This option trading strategy requires the investor or trader to move or roll the strike point when the option expires. The term rolling is derived from this type of trading strategy. On the other hand, traders and investors need to make sure their strategy provides them with a means to stop or avoid rolling when it is not in their best interest to continue.

If a trader or investor decides not to roll the strike point, then they are allowing their investment to increase or appreciate. This is not a normal strategy to use with options trading, but it can be a transaction utilized if the market conditions warrant this type of option trading. In this case when the option is exercised, and the share is turned into capital, it could be called away.

In options trading when an option is expiring, the trader or investor can perform one of two types of transactions. They can execute a short option, which refers to being 'out of the money' or 'in the money.' If the option is 'out of the money,' then it is essentially worthless. In this case, the trader or investor will sell the next month's call after letting the option expire. If the option is 'on the money,' then the trader or investor needs to sell the next month's call after repurchasing the short option to keep the stock. Even thought that type of trade is two trades, buying and selling, it is considered one trade. This is also known as a spread. To roll out your covered call or buy-write, you need to utilize this type of spread so you can buy back the short option and keep your stock.

To maintain your covered call strategy traders would sell their second-month option short. The remaining positions are long stock and short calls that traders and investors then buy back at the beginning of each month with no choice on front month options. There are choices to sell near term or with a further expiration date for the next month option using this type of option trading strategy. However, rolling options can be complicated and best left to experienced traders and investors to avoid unnecessary investment risks.

I am sure we would all like to make a lot of money with the best option trading ideas. In fact, some concepts and methods can be implemented using a small options trading account, for example, using a $,2000 account, and risking $300 - $500 on single, selective, and fair probability trades. These are the trades that would have a smaller probability of going well, than the rest we usually do, but they can often have a huge profit potential. And I mean huge beyond anything you can imagine!

We are going to discuss two such high-profit potential concepts and one small profit potential concept. They are all considered low budget option trading ideas and can be implemented using ATM or OTM options.

1. Capturing company mergers and acquisitions phases
2. Capturing technical momentum breakouts
3. Ways to trade OTM options in high probability setups

Let's see them in detail, concept 1 is well known, but is it possible to know where the next merger will occur? The fact is that most of the mergers happen during market tops and bottoms, they don't happen as often in any other period. In fact, the vast majority of companies, do that! During market tops and bottoms, so you only have to watch out just before that major market top or bottom. That is the top of a bull market and the bottom of a bear market, but there are also, other rare cases in between, where a merger may be detected.

It takes a lot of research, fundamental research, and market savvy to figure out what weak balance sheet companies could merge with what strong companies. And how they see mutual benefits. If you can't do it yourself, you can still find experts who perform this fundamental analysis, follow the news closely, and could provide you with the list of the favorable candidates.

Beyond that, you should also understand yourself how this works, for example: what if company A merges with Company B? And if A is much bigger and stronger than B, then B's stock price will skyrocket! And not only you can buy B's stock at a low price, but if the merger is set to take place during a bear market bottom, then both the stocks of A and B will be significantly lower than their actual intrinsic value, or just way lower than their five-year highs!

Actual profit potential on company mergers is enormous, sometimes you can turn $500 into $30,000 by just buying a cheap ATM or OTM Call option! It may sound like a long shot bet, but it doesn't have to be like that! You can increase the probability of winning by doing your research at the right time and on the most likely candidate stocks. That way you know, that you are getting the odds on your side, even if you place a series of 10 trades, at $500 each, and eight trades lose say 50% of their value because of the merger plans being canceled, you can still make a fortune on the remaining two!

If we assume you lose a total of $2,000 on the trades gone bad, and this is a worst case scenario! You still get two mergers right, and you get in early in the options trade, what if these two trades make a 20fold gain on your $500 option trade? You get back $20,000 from these two accurate trades!

This technique is possible and requires a lot of market savvy in analyzing and monitoring company news and their business outlook.

Then we have technique number 2, capturing technical momentum that is about to be released. Well, believe it or not, most of the time, high volume, quality stocks whose companies are about to merge, DO produce technical indications on the charts. These indications are foretelling of a huge breakout to occur, even though we cannot be so sure about the direction, with a little bit of more digging into the news and fundamentals we can gain more insight as to what the most likely scenario is.

Please be aware that option brokers are the market makers here; they will use all information available to price their option premiums. The good news is that they can only use what is out there, and as we have seen, the options pricing formula uses stock parameters that are merely a story about the past. In no way does imply volatility accurately predict stock price fluctuation, it does provide accuracy on average, and over 1000's of stocks, so that option brokers adjust the premiums at a fair price. Call options sellers (From whom you will buy your Call option) will be paid a reasonable premium.

But this doesn't mean they cannot be completely wrong on a single stock, of course, they can be wrong!

This is like car insurance companies, their insurance premiums are calculated to protect the company against the average expected loss, and sure the company will never lose money in the long term. But they cannot predict and pinpoint the driver that will make the next massive claim, neither are they clever enough to identify the number of fraudulent claims some savvy car drivers successfully make!

Statistics work collectively, but is not a crystal ball! And the option pricing formula often gets caught, completely off guard when a technical breakout occurs, that is because this formula doesn't take the technical analysis into account!

In fact, some people and some academics don't believe in technical analysis at all.

For the rest of us who do believe in technical analysis, we have seen it very often, proving market makers and their option premiums wrong!

Check out this simple triangle formation on the Microsoft stock (MSFT), this pattern is a very reliable breakout pattern, and the options pricing formula does not see it:

In such cases, or even other even more dramatic cases, you can buy cheap ATM options, and make a very good profit. The option market makers will offer you a cheap ATM option, or even a cheap OTM option. In the above case of Microsoft, an OTM option could be cheap and have a Delta of around 10. A Delta of 10 means that the option will only make $0.10 for every $1 the stock moves higher, up until it becomes ITM. A Delta of 10 also tells you that they believe this option has a 10% probability of expiring in-the-money, and it may sound discouraging, almost like a lottery ticket. But the technical analysis picture above tells me that the stock will prevail over the option pricing formula and the low Delta! The only thing I need is enough price movement.

This is just an event of uneven probability, (event A is far more likely than event B) here we know that they have kept premiums low, even though we know volatility will breakout soon, and I also know the stock will most likely go up. I can therefore profit from this move by risking a very small amount of money!

Again, as I mentioned, these opportunities emerge here and there, every day in the markets. The probability is there, to outsmart the market makers by profiting big, from a cheap option. Like I said, from an opportunity perspective, it's equivalent to fooling a car insurance company and making a fraudulent claim, one that their experts cannot understand.

Bear in mind that Mergers and Technical breakouts can sometimes coincide, you may get technical confirmation of the suspected merger, even though we treat them separately!

By observing implied and historical volatilities, using Anlayzetrade.com back testing tools, one can sell OTM options when these are the most expensive, and then buy them back when they become cheaper (When implied volatility is low compared to implied volatility range, and historical volatility range)

Selling options is not a low budget strategy, but there are ways and strategies that take care of this by implementing protection, (covered option writing).

Where the trader finds the opportunity to write options, then also finds a trade to hedge this risk just to minimize the margin requirements of the broker, and make it indeed a low budget selling strategy.

For example, we have seen Calendar spreads, where you can profit from the fast time decaying option while staying protected from moderate adverse moves. This eliminates the need of a large account size. But we can also devise trades where the objective is to profit from the underlying stock's move while being sellers. Again popular ideas are not very profitable or smart. You still need stock-specific, technical analysis based strategies. But they do work! And Analyzetrade.com offers just the tools required to develop these strategies. The objective here is to write ITM options of high value, that will become OTM and cheap, within few days.

Related Keywords:

option strategies, options strategies, stock options trading, put call ratio, trade options, option trade, best trading software, stock option software, option strategy, option trader, call option, put option, option trading system, options strategy, option price, stock option strategy, option trades, real time trading, stock option trading software, stock option strategies, trend trading software, options trades, option pricing strategies, future and option trading, stock option trading strategy,

Stock options software,

stock options strategies,

Anyone at all involved in investing or trading no doubt personally experienced it- the stock markets went through a major correction! And in these days of the "World Economy," such a correction can be triggered by news from anywhere in the world. As it did this time. Poor economic news from China prompted a sharp world decline in stock prices in just a few days.

And many investors, especially long term investors made big losses.

And they're probably asking:

"Is there some way I could have avoided making losses during that period?"

Well, the answer is absolute Yes.

Obviously trying to predict such a correction and get out before it happens is extremely difficult, and honestly more a matter of luck than anything else.

But by diversifying your trading strategies you can avoid losses during such times - and in fact, make healthy profits instead!

The key is to employ a mix of trading techniques that take advantage of a variety of trading time frames.

Avoid putting all your eggs in the "long term" basket and look at complementing your trading with styles that make returns over the shorter term as well:

- Swing trading is an excellent way to capitalize on market movements over a period of just a few days or weeks.

- Day trading, of course, allows you to make returns on stock movements within just one day.

And, mix up how and what you trade:

- Include Short Selling in your trading techniques. By selling a stock or index short, you are looking to profit from downward moves. This is just as valid as trying to buy low and sell high. And offers an important hedge against a market correction

- Also, there are now Inverse and even Double-Inverse indices that can be traced quite easily. DOG is the symbol for the Inverse Dow 30 Index and DXD are the Double Inverse Dow 30. By owning these, you are essentially short selling the major stock indices.

And, contrary to popular belief, it is not difficult to begin trading in this manner.

SIMPLE DAY TRADING STRATEGIES

Over the years online trading has exploded in popularity and, as a result, the resources, tools, strategies, and infrastructure available to the ordinary investor have become enormous.

- Online brokers offer trading accounts with extremely low commissions that allow investors to trade all kinds of different instruments (stocks, options, futures, forex) over all kinds of different timeframes (day trading, swing trading, long term trading).

- A large number of trading strategies and systems are also available online. And many such systems, offer a spectrum of short term and longer term strategies in a single service.

- And online trading platforms have become very sophisticated, offering complex analysis tools and even the ability to develop and back test trading strategies.

So, what simple steps can you take to profit during rising markets AND market corrections?

- Long Term trading: Allocate a portion of your trading funds to long term investments (over many months). Make your profits from the overall market trends - remember to take those profits periodically so that a sudden downturn does not catch you. And look to include some of those Inverse Indices in your portfolio. They can act as a tremendous hedge against market corrections.

- Medium Term trading: Allocate a portion of your trading funds to Swing Trading. In this way, you capitalize on the medium term trends in the markets or individual stocks. Practically all financial instruments go through these medium term swings as traders are constantly trying to determine the right longer term price by buying and selling at support and resistance levels. And by taking both long and Short trades on these swings, you stand to profit in both directions!

- Short Term trading: Allocate a portion of your trading funds to Day Trading. This allows you to completely take the longer term market factors out of the equation. By trading within a single day, it doesn't matter that there was a long term correction. You profit anyway. With the right strategy, you would undoubtedly recognize the selling opportunity presented on the day(s) when there is a market correction. And by selling short, you stand to make enormous gains that day!

Stock trading is carried out by stock traders who for the most part need an intermediate such as a brokerage firm or bank to perform the trades. Stock traders work for themselves by investing money in shares which they believe will increase in value over time and then sell the shares at a later date for profit.

There are some strategies used by stock traders to accumulate profit. The most popular stock trading strategies are day trading, swing trading, value investing and growth trading. A brief description of each of these strategies will now be given

* Day trading is a form of trading in which stocks are sold and bought during a single day so that at the end of the day there is no change in the number of shares held. This is done by selling a share each time another share of equivalent value is bought. The profit or loss comes from the difference between the sale price and the purchasing price of the share. The motivation behind day trading is to avoid any overnight shocks that might occur in stock markets. All stocks are held for a very short period

* Swing traders hold stocks over a medium period, say a couple of days or 1 or 2 weeks. Swing traders usually trade with stocks that are actively traded. These stocks swing between a very general high and low extreme. Swing traders must, therefore, purchase stocks at the low end of their value and then sell the shares when they swing back up.

* Value investing is a method of stock trading in which traders purchase shares in a company which they consider to have underpriced shares. The hope is that by investing in the company, the shares will eventually increase in value.

* Growth investing is a method of investing in companies that are showing signs of above average growth. The share price may be higher than what it would be expected to be however the view of the trader is that the share value will grow into what it has been purchased for.

Stock trading does come at a cost, however. The high levels of risk and uncertainty, as well as the complex nature of stock trading, is enough to deter most people from becoming stock traders. There is also the brokerage fee charged by the bank or the brokerage firm every time a transaction is carried out. However all this aside there is still a considerable chance of getting lucky as a stock trader which is enough to supply the stock trading industry for the foreseeable future.

Stock Trading Strategies - Do You Know These Simple Yet Highly Profitable Strategies For Trading Stocks?

Stock trading is carried out by stock traders who for the most part need an intermediate such as a brokerage firm or bank to perform the trades. Stock traders work for themselves by investing money in shares which they believe will increase in value over time and then sell the shares at a later date for profit.

There are some strategies used by stock traders to accumulate profit. The most popular stock trading strategies are day trading, swing trading, value investing and growth trading. A brief description of each of these strategies will now be given

* Day trading is a form of trading in which stocks are sold and bought during a single day so that at the end of the day there is no change in the number of shares held. This is done by selling a share each time another share of equivalent value is bought. The profit or loss comes from the difference between the sale price and the purchasing price of the share. The motivation behind day trading is to avoid any overnight shocks that might occur on stock markets. All stocks are held for a very short period

* Swing traders hold stocks over a medium period, say a couple of days or 1 or 2 weeks. Swing traders usually trade with stocks that are actively traded. These stocks swing between a very general high and low extreme. Swing traders must, therefore, purchase stocks at the low end of their value and then sell the shares when they swing back up.

* Value investing is a method of stock trading in which traders purchase shares in a company which they consider to have underpriced shares. The hope is that by investing in the company, the shares will eventually increase in value.

* Growth investing is a method of investing in companies that are showing signs of above average growth. The share price may be

higher than what it would be expected to be however the view of the trade is that the share value will grow into what it has been purchased for.

Stock trading does come at a cost, however. The high levels of risk and uncertainty, as well as the complex nature of stock trading, is enough to deter most people from becoming stock traders. There is also the brokerage fee charged by the bank or the brokerage firm every time a transaction is carried out.

However all this aside there is still a considerable chance of getting lucky as a stock trader which is enough to supply the stock trading industry for the foreseeable future?

Chapter 2

ONLINE TRADING STRATEGY.

Online stock trading is an easy way of buying and selling stocks online using an online stock broker. Since stock markets are highly volatile and sensitive markets, you are required to strategize every move you make regarding buying and selling of stocks. For new comers, it becomes ever more essential to be cautious and follow certain online stock trading strategies.

Conventionally, you are required to give a call to your broker, giving him or her instructions as to what you want to trade in. But the advent of the internet has simplified this, and now you can trade in stocks online at your will and discretion. Every stock broker cannot be trusted to make financial decisions on your part as most of them are simply sales agents who have been handed over a stock list from their seniors and told to persuade their clients to buy or sell them.

Now the question arises as to which online stock trading strategies should be followed to get a reliable broker. It is usually a big ask as there is no dearth of them to choose from. Hence, you need to be vigilant. Look for a reputed and major broker that owns huge assets. You do not want your broker to get into bankruptcy.

One of the online stock trading strategies is to seek some information from prospective brokerage agencies, asking them a few questions so that you can make the right choice. Ask them what the minimum amount that you should invest to start online trading is and whether any fee will be charged for inactivity. Inquire about trading commissions for stocks and the type of trading guidance you need.

You must follow online stock trading strategies seriously. As it is a business, you need to educate yourself on different aspects of stock trading, prepare your funding amount, and plan carefully. Don't try to become a millionaire in a single day.

Judicious online stock trading strategies demand that you are disciplined, skillful, and trade according to a plan. If you are serious about this trade, then and only then you should plunge into the online stock trading market.

The arena of online trading stock and option is quite an extensive one, with many options for you to choose from. Since its inception, many part time and casual investors have been borne from the ease of access to some markets due to their partnership with online companies and the resources of the internet. There are also many companies that are starting to offer services basic and advanced that will fit the trader out there.

Over the time spent doing your research, you will notice that there is a ton of information and you need to be discerning when picking and choosing your markets, the commodity and of course which financial institution you attach yourself to. Then and only then will you be making an informed decision on your investment portfolio. One of the things you will need to factor into your investment market decision is, of course, the cost per trade that you will either incur or benefit from once you have chosen your commodity. A lot of stock companies online have many systems of inventive and offers that they will give to you once you do a certain volume of trades on a very regular basis.

This can be as little as $1 a trade or as high as $50 a trade, depending on the volume, and while it may seem like a paltry amount at first, but soon the amounts will be adding up, and they will make a difference in your capital management. How much they charge per trade is also important and the figures could easily add up to feel your strategies within weeks.

Look out for companies that charge low on their trades, and they are quite easy to find on the web - this is a good choice especially for beginner traders who are not too familiar with the market and need time to acclimatize to the situation. Secondly, you also need to attach yourself to a company of some repute, which means you simply cannot just choose the first one you see. You do not want to be in the position of sending large amounts of money to a company and realizing that they have been squandering it away with bad investment decisions all the time.

Check with governing resources, financial institutions that do regular checks on such companies and best of all - check the feedback system the internet naturally reproduces to get some unsolicited customer feedback on the products and their services. Thirdly, you also need to is the interface that you will eventually be provided with is simple and easy to navigate. Investing and predicting market movements is already a tricky job as it is, but then you cannot be put in a position where you are juggling with many other complicated and complex issues with the interface system. With these things in mind, you should be well on your way to making full use of online trading stock and option to its potential and start amassing some real cash.

SIMPLE DAY TRADING STRATEGIES

An intelligent trader once said, `The only difference between gambling at a casino and day trading stock online is that you have to serve yourself drinks when sitting at your home computer.`

Sure... some day traders have made some decent money through day trading stock online. But these are the exception, not the rule. Most day traders lose in the long run and that `long run` isn't too long at times!

You see, the trouble is... most day traders are seeking a `quick fix`. Their persona isn`t suited to midterm or long term trading. They quite likely have lost money in the past, either through gambling of some sort or through losing patience with longer term trading strategies that turned sour. They most likely don`t have a large capital base, especially if they`ve been wiped out a few times in the past. And so the concept of... day trading stock online is incredibly appealing.

Unfortunately, far too many traders who`ve either made the switch to day trading - or who are brand spanking new to it and thereby lack basic risk management skills.

For one thing, seduced by the apparent simplicity of it all, many traders approach the whole thing of day trading stock online without really knowing what they`re doing. Secondly, they have little or no concept of the underlying risks involved. Thirdly, as I`ve already alluded to, they often find themselves ` undercapitalized`. Fourthly, and most definitely a deal-killer...

They play with borrowed funds!

Not a good move... and a breach of fundamental trading basics to boot!

So, is it even possible to make a living from day trading stock online?

Yes, it is. But the odds are stacked against you from day one. You positively HAVE TO HAVE A PLAN... or you`ll lose... simple as that.

For starters... you have to know your entry and exit points BEFORE entering the market. It`s no good waiting until the market has moved so far against you that you`re too frightened to take the loss! When you participate in day trading stock online, you have to leave your emotions at the door and follow your plan like your life depends on it (which some might argue `it does`).

Suppose you buy 1,000 shares of ABC-XYZ at $1 per share - on a day trading basis... and you notice that the stock rises 30 cents a share before lunch. The left-side of your brain coolly advises you to `get out and pocket a massive $300 profit`. Hells bells... 30% in the morning is a good earn!

However, you also have this other side of your brain which has no basis in logic.. It is commonly referred to as the `emotional side` or right-side of your brain. It also has a deeply embedded relationship with every gambler`s nemesis... `Greed`. Accordingly, you decide in your professional lack of wisdom to... `Just hold on in there a little longer... it`s bound to go higher`.

You go out and make some lunch, have a coffee... and smile...in the knowledge that you`re a day trading wizard who is on the brink of making a fortune. And it`s all so damn easy!

1.45pm...

The stock has reached intraday highs of $1.37... `Maybe it`ll hit $1.50 by closing bell?`

2.52pm...

The news comes out that the company`s patent is invalid... the stock plunges to $0.60 in three minutes...

For you, the dream has not only been shattered, but the sky has just fallen in... and your $1,000 investment has reversed a $337 profit into a $400 loss... and it`s still falling.

You find yourself hurled into a maelstrom of helplessness, fear, and chaos...but with no plan in place; you simply hang on in there.

3.30 pm...

Trading in the stock is suspended. The last trade went through at $0.42. You are so stunned you can`t even shed a tear. Your day trading career lasted precisely 6 hours, 22 minutes and 8 seconds...

`Welcome to the frenetic world of... day trading stock online`.

For some of you, this article may very well bring back some rather painful memories. For others, let it be a warning...

If day trading stock online is something that you are serious about and want to succeed in, then at least show you`ve got the intelligence, emotional control, and discipline to survive the bad hits as well as bagging the big profits!

There are over 10,000,000 web pages in Google dealing with courses and coaching on the subject of day trading stock online. So, before you risk another cent... do yourself (and your bank account) a favor… and start researching the mentoring options out there… until you find one that suits.

Fortunately for beginners, there are numerous methods available to learn the basics of online trading:

Books – both hard-copy and e-books are available that guide you through your investment decisions and how to pick both investments and a broker.

Online sources – just perform a couple of searches on the internet and you can find thousands of companies and individuals with a wealth of information and guidance for you. A word of caution – as in any business endeavor there are unscrupulous resources just waiting to take advantage of inexperienced or naïve individuals. Check credentials before proceeding with these contacts. One well-known source of investing information is investopia.com.

Personal mentors – perhaps you know a friend or family member who is familiar with online stock trading. Their experience can be invaluable to you with guidance on what has worked for them and what strategies failed them. Due your due diligence on any "hot tips" provided though.

Study – before investing it is important to understand the company or vehicle you're investing in. Do some research on the company and its recent stock trend and earnings potential? Some of the most successful investors such as Peter Lynch have suggested that investors participate in what they know. This means that if you have in-depth knowledge of a market such as health care or commodities such as metals or agriculture products it may be to your advantage to invest in markets that you understand.

Monitor news and company announcements – when companies announce financial events such as restructuring, earnings expectations, or looming layoffs it will impact your investment decisions. Global news events such as political unrest or economic conditions will similarly impact stock markets, possibly with either for short-term or long-term results. There are many excellent sources for news including CNN.

Experience – once you have selected an online stock broker, start slow. Don't risk considerable capital with your first trade however lucrative it may appear on the surface. Remember that all capital is at risk in the stock market. Don't participate in markets that you have no understanding of such as stock futures until you've had time to truly feel comfortable with such vehicles.

Learn how to read stock charts – there are multiple forms of stock charts investors utilize to track stock performance and market trends. Some are reasonably basic for use by beginners, and others are extremely complex that tend to be utilized by more experienced savvy investors. Stockcarts.com is a good site for beginning chart reference. At the least get a basic understanding of standard stock ticker information that's available on nearly every financial page or brokerage site.

Learning Online Stock Trading in a Nutshell

Once you've decided that online stock trading is right for you the steps to successful trading are:

Get a computer with internet access (some online brokers also support a tablet or smartphone)

Set up an online brokerage account

Determine the investment strategy that you will pursue (stocks, commodities, etc.)

Research market conditions and news sources for the right timing to buy a particular stock

Make that first buy order

Continue monitoring your investment for the indicators revealing the right time to sell. Note that day traders monitor these conditions closely and may hold an investment for only a few days, hours, or even minutes.

Keep notes – keep a ledger of what strategy worked – and did not. It's your experience that will allow you to fine-tune and adjust your investment strategy. You learn as much from your failures and your successes.

Getting Started with Online Stock Trading

Once you've made your determination on the investment instruments that most fit your trading strategy and loss tolerance you need to select an online broker. It's your online broker that will facilitate your research and execute your buy and sell orders. Be certain the online broker you select has the features you need for analysis and monitoring of the stocks you're interested in. Online brokers may vary in the financial products they offer to clients. To maximize your investment options be sure your broker provides a full complement that includes stocks, bonds, commodities, and forex trading.

Sure Trader is a leading online broker with the tools and news access that keeps day traders informed of market trends and conditions that can impact decisions and timing for buying and selling. This provides traders with the ability to react swiftly to take advantage of financial opportunities across national and global markets. Utilization of Sure Trader's sophisticated technology facilitates the quick decisions and lightning-fast trades that make you successful. Desktop and mobile applications ensure timely access to Sure Trader services – smartphone access is provided for both iOS and Android platforms. Investors can rely on friendly and courteous support 24×7 to allow execution of trades quickly and efficiently even in after-hours trading.

Chapter 3

STOCK TRADING SERVICES.

One of the best ways to boost your finances is to make smart investments and to manage those investments wisely. This used to mean hiring a good broker, but in today's world, there are many options for stock trading services that enable people to manage an investment portfolio yourself.

Whether you're just beginning to manage your investments or you're a seasoned expert, it's important to choose an online stock trading service that will provide you with all the data and analytical tools you need to make well-informed financial decisions. The best online services will also be easy to use and offer plenty of resources to help you understand the trading process.

The Top Ten REVIEWS has done extensive research on online stock trading services. The site also has a stock trading configurator to help you determine which trading option is best for you. Here are the top three recommendations for online stock trading services:

1. Options Xpress by Charles Schwab

This service wins the top seat for its advanced trading tools, easily understood fee schedule, and low margin rate. Options press excels at providing lots of stock data and educational information for traders at a reasonable price.

Investments Offered: Options press has many options when it comes to investments, including stocks, mutual funds, exchange-traded funds, and bonds. This service also offers IRAs to retirement and education savings plans.

Trading Tools: This service provides a wide range of tools and educational resources to facilitate your trading and investment. From calculators and charts to streaming news and analyst research reports, this site has you covered regarding information?

Cost: To compare the cost of this service with others like it, visit Top Ten REVIEWS' best online stock trading services comparisons and reviews here.

2. Options House

Options House takes second place for its commitment to educating traders, reasonable fees and commissions, good customer support, and user-friendly trading platform.

Investments Offered: This service offers both stock and options trading, as well as bonds. It also provides access to a range of mutual and retirement funds.

Trading Tools: Options House offers a wide array of tools and resources, including probability and profit calculators, Call Spread and Covered Call Investigators, and applications for live-streaming news.

Trade King offers all the basic tools for investment, including calculators, graphs, charts, and streaming news. It also provides a plethora of educational materials for your perusal, including web tutorials and podcasts.

Cost

To compare the cost of this service with others like it, visit Top Ten REVIEWS' best online stock trading services comparisons and reviews here.

Trade King

Trade King garners a good review for its exceptional customer service, amazingly low prices, and commitment to client education.

Investments Offered: This service offers stocks, options, mutual funds, and exchange-traded funds. It also offers fixed income investments like bonds and CDs, though these orders must be made via telephone. Trade King provides access to IRA accounts for retirement and education savings.

Some online trading services provide financial services, which are comparable to what a bank would offer but the annual percentage rates offered on certificates of deposit, are noticeably better because the rate is higher. The high yields attained on a yearly basis on these type of cash building devices can entice many investors to transact all online trades with that specific trading service available online.

With a trading account on the web, it is possible for investors to access many online wealth-building programs. These trading services provide members with opportunities to participate in global trades, where over six markets exist that will earn investors top dollar on monies invested in the foreign currency trading practices of countries all over the world. The wealth building strategies for trading in currencies is one of the factors that make online traders part of global commerce.

The online trading services that investors are most interested in when they log in to an online service providers website through the internet are services normally found in a bank. These trading services primarily deal with providing stock and other financial trading options to investors, but many take advantage of the high rates on saving accounts. The investment services offered throughout the year are a great way for investors to maintain a competitive edge in the future.

Trading services such as investing allow people to manage individual retirement accounts through a virtual banker. Some trading services will place large amounts of money into a retirement account just to get customers started on the right path of saving for retirement. An online investor can take care of all types of business transactions while online because online banking is one of the services that are provided.

Investors feel that they get a much-needed break from trading fees when they use the trading service provider's services online. These fees can cost an investor lots of cash each day, especially when they are trading more than 100 or more stocks each week, and more if the stock market climate dictates it. As a reward for establishing a trading account with a particular trading service provider, some investors are gifted over 100 trades that are free of any commission charges when they are finally sold.

Online trading service providers that know how to be smart where profits are concerned usually employ a broker that offers premium services. The most intelligent brokers are always active when it comes to trading and will also be the people responsible for keeping tabs on the pulse of the commodities markets too. To be able to provide all trading services well, it takes a well-rounded broker who is knowledgeable in all aspects of online trading and the climate of trades being made around the world.

The wise investor will use all of the trading services available at their disposal because that is where the smart money can be accessed through online trading deals. Some of the services provided will help in retirement planning, and others will provide investors with advice and an education on all active trading practices so that all online trading matters are positive and profitable for everyone.

We all revolve around the internet. We communicate, work, and get entertained by the internet; it's a cyber world where we can all exist and can be whatever we can be and do whatever we'd like to do. It is so popular that almost everything can be done through it. People work and find jobs through the internet; forget about the telephone because we all get in touch with friends and families through the internet; people interact and share thoughts through the internet, and now food delivery is available through the internet

One of the best benefits of the internet is the availability of online trading services. So who uses this and why is it so important. As said earlier, the internet is a world of its own and people work in it. People from all over the world work for clients that communicate and create transactions through the internet and because of this even the payment transactions are done online. Since the employer and the employee come from opposite ends of the world, most likely payments are done in different currencies. This is where online trading websites come in, and some of the benefits that they provide include:

Convenience

This is the most obvious reason why a lot of people prefer to do online transactions is that of convenience and ease in the transaction. Equipped with fast and efficient internet access, you can make payments and transact at any time, in any place. Whether you're at the office, at home, in the library, or using your smart phone, you can easily make the necessary transactions through online trading websites.

Time is also not an issue when it comes to online foreign currency exchange. You can make your transactions at any time of the day, and it doesn't matter if it's night time or day time. As long your internet speed is good, it's open for service 24 hours a day, seven days a week.

Better Money Returns

There are a lot of foreign currency exchange websites on the internet, all of them work perfectly well, but the only challenge for you is to find the one with the best exchange rate. Once you get the right website, you will be able to get better money returns and higher exchange rates. The internet is home to so many information and sources when it comes to foreign currency exchange, all you have to do is to find the one with better returns.

Cheaper costs and lesser fees

Most people prefer to choose online trading websites since these sites charge minimal fees and can help you get a higher exchange rate. Also, most online trade websites charge zero exchange fees which also results in a higher conversion.

There is thousand type of business available in the world, and people assume what will suitable for them. When the time comes to the business of trading, taking profits in commodities is one of the more important aspects. Maximum times it is observed that the beginners are always in conflict with the emotions of fear and greed when the time comes for taking profits. According to experts, a successful commodity trader will avoid both and use a more structured means of making profits.

Before taking the profits, traders need to plan thoroughly that which is the right time to take profits from the trade and how much they plan on risking on a trade before the trade is even placed. It doesn't mean that a trader knows all the things and the exact price on the risk and profit levels. A trader may have a set of rules where he or she could plan to exit from trade. If the given conditions met, then the trader will take profits on that trade.

Furthermore, there are some traders those are following different ways to let the profits run until the market reverses. For instance, a commodity trader could buy gold futures and can hold on until the bellow point of the market. On the market moves below, the trader will have to exit the positions no matter whether it is a win, lose or draw. Sometimes, there are some traders those used fixed dollar amount to take profits on all their trades. This is one of the easiest ways to trade without thinking much about the existing level.

Sometimes grabbing profits, at major supporter or resistance level are considered as the most logical types of options to use. Sometimes, support and resistance points are eventually broken, but the odds are that they will hold. For this reason, maximum commodity traders will take the profits before market tests these levels.

The most important thing is that taking profits is the best have to plan before traders are placed. If a trader has the lack of profit objective, then it'll leave him to uncertainty and mounting stress. This will often lead to poor decision making and constant second guessing. After all, there are some best trade finance companies those are providing all type of assistance that you always needed for your trade and even Swiss company incorporation is there to assist you from all angle that you always need.

So now the question is that how to find the best trade finance service, provider? The Internet is the best medium to know about them, and you should choose them according to their reputation and ability to handle the matter. So browse the internet today and get the best one.

Chapter 4

RISK MANAGEMENT IN STOCK TRADING.

Successful traders understand the importance of risk management. Trading is inherently risky because it is a zero sum game. Every dollar you gain through trading represents a loss on someone else's balance sheet. Traders win and lose in the financial markets every day. The difference between successful and not-so-successful traders is understanding and applying a simple risk management strategy.

While risk management is a broad topic, it means one thing for our purposes here. Namely, to "cut your losses early."

Write it down and put this phrase somewhere near your trading station. It is the difference between making a nice income from trading and from losing your shirt.

A losing trader has no trading plan. He hears about a stock that is destined to go up in value, so he buys. Then the stock tanks about 10% and then he buys more. After all, now it's on "sale" right? Then, the price goes down even more, and the losing trader buys even more. This guy is paying for his ticket to the poorhouse. He has no business trading stocks because he is aimless in his pursuits.

Pride is the number one reason that traders lose big money in the markets. If you can learn early in your trading career to admit when you have a loser on your hands and sell, you can go far. If a stock trade doesn't work out the way that you had planned, sell the stock. There is nothing wrong with losing money on a trade. It happens every day. Instead, view your losses as your "tuition" on Wall Street. Learn from your mistakes and try to avoid repeating them.

Know Your "Exit" Before You "Enter."

Successful traders create their risk management strategy by determining up front how much money they are willing to lose on each given trade. In other words, before you place a trade to buy a stock, you need to set your maximum risk. Are you willing to lose 50% if the stock goes south? I hope not. That's another sure ticket to the poor house.

Here are some of the most common questions that I received over the years from new traders. My answers are always the same.

Q: So how do you know when it's time to sell a stock that is falling in price?

A: This is a question that only you can answer because everyone has a different tolerance for risk.

Q: How do you decide your exit in advance of your entry?

A: By creating your own pre-determined set of risk management rules.

Q: How much of loss should you take before you decide to liquidate your position within a stock?

A: It depends upon your purpose for the trade and your tolerance for risk.

My point is simple: You must own your success and your mistakes. Other people do not get to tell you when to sell. As a trader, that is your domain. As you can see, there are no hard and fast rules on these matters.

To me, "cutting your losses early" means just that... early. I don't like to lose money, and my tolerance for risk has decreased over the years. Therefore, my experience and my preferences impact my definition of that word "early." And while I cannot tell you what your risk management strategy should be, I will share mine with you. Perhaps you can take mine and use it as a template to formulate your risk management strategy.

Risk management is an essential but often overlooked prerequisite to successful active trading. After all, a trader who has generated substantial profits over his or her lifetime can lose it all in just one or two bad trades if proper risk management isn't employed. This article will discuss some simple strategies that can be used to protect your trading profits.

Planning Your Trades

As Chinese military general Sun Tzu's famously said: "Every battle is won before it is fought." The phrase implies that planning and strategy - not the battles - win wars. Similarly, successful traders commonly quote the phrase: "Plan the trade and trade the plan." Just like in war, planning can often mean the difference between success and failure.

Stop-loss (S/L) and take-profit (T/P) points represent two key ways in which traders can plan when trading. Successful traders know what price they are willing to pay and at what price they are willing to sell, and they measure the resulting returns against the probability of the stock hitting their goals. If the adjusted return is high enough, then they execute the trade.

Conversely, unsuccessful traders often enter a trade without having any idea of the points at which they will sell at a profit or a loss. Like gamblers on a lucky or unlucky streak, emotions begin to take over and dictate their trades. Losses often provoke people to hold on and hope to make their money back, while profits often entice traders to hold on for even more gains imprudently.

Stop-Loss and Take-Profit Points

A stop-loss point is a price at which a trader will sell a stock and take a loss on the trade. Often this happens when a trade does not pan out the way a trader hoped. The points are designed to prevent the "it will come back" mentality and limit losses before they escalate. For example, if a stock breaks below a key support level, traders often sell as soon as possible.

On the other side of the table, a take-profit point is a price at which a trader will sell a stock and take a profit on the trade. Often this is when the additional upside is limited given the risks. For example, if a stock is approaching a key resistance level after a large move upward, traders may want to sell before a period of consolidation takes place.

How to Effectively Set Stop-Loss Points

Setting stop-loss and take-profit points are often done using technical analysis, but the fundamental analysis can also play a key role in timing. For example, if a trader is holding a stock ahead of earnings as excitement builds, he or she may want to sell before the news hits the market if expectations have become too high, regardless of whether the take-profit price was hit.

Moving averages represent the most popular way to set these points, as they are easy to calculate and widely tracked by the market. Key moving averages include the five-, nine-, 20-, 50-, 100- and 200-day averages. These are best set by applying them to a stock's chart and determining whether the stock price has reacted to them in the past as either support or resistance level.

Another great way to place stop-loss or take-profit levels is on support or resistance trendiness. These can be drawn by connecting previous highs or lows that occurred on significant, above-average volume. Just like moving averages, the key is determining levels at which the price reacts to the trend lines, and of course, with high volume.

When setting these points, here are some key considerations:

Use longer-term moving averages for more volatile stocks to reduce the chance that a meaningless price swing will trigger a stop-loss order to be executed.

Adjust the moving averages to match target price ranges; for example, longer targets should use larger moving averages to reduce the number of signals generated.

Stop losses should not be closer than 1.5-times the current high-to-low range (volatility), as it is too likely to get executed without reason.

Adjust the stop loss according to the market's volatility; if the stock price isn't moving too much, then the stop-loss points can be tightened.

Use known fundamental events, such as earnings releases, as key time periods to be in or out of a trade as volatility and uncertainty can rise.

Calculating Expected Return

Setting stop-loss and take-profit points are also necessary to calculate expected the return. The importance of this calculation cannot be overstated, as it forces traders to think through their trades and rationalize them. As well, it gives them a systematic way to compare various deals and select only the most profitable ones.

This can be calculated using the following formula:

[(Probability of Gain) x (Take Profit % Gain)] + [(Probability of Loss) x (Stop Loss % Loss)]

The result of this calculation is an expected return for the active trader, who will then measure it against other opportunities to determine which stocks to trade. The probability of gain or loss can be calculated by using historical breakouts and breakdowns from the support or resistance levels; or for experienced traders, by making an educated guess.

The Bottom Line

Traders should always know when they plan to enter or exit a trade before they execute. By using stop losses effectively, a trader can minimize not only losses but also the number of times a trade is exited needlessly. Make your battle plan of time, so you'll already know you've won the war.

All businesses have inherent risks attached.

A shop owner may have to consider the risk of produce being left unsold on the shelf, the possibility that key staff leave for pastures new, electricity supply gets disrupted, or tax laws change. Or a whole host of other possible risks to his business.

To alleviate such risks he may cut prices, initiating sales periods, or hold key persons insurance or have a staff lending and borrowing policy with a nearby store in the same chain. He might have a back-up generator, and will most definitely employ an accountant.

In other words, he manages his risk on a daily and ongoing basis. He identifies areas of risk, assesses impact, and then prioritizes necessary remedial action.

As a stock trader, you'll need to do the same. By managing the risk associated with your portfolio, you'll increase your chances of increasing profits, and decrease your chances of being hit hard by the unexpected. There are several areas in which you need to identify and assess your risk, and several things you can do manage that risk successfully.

Position Size

Unless you're Warren Buffet, you will have a finite fund to commit to the markets. You'll need to consider the size of this fund, the anticipated (or required) profit, and the potential loss. It's no good committing all of your funds, if to do so would jeopardize future trading.

Many active traders set a limit on the maximum risk they will take per trade. For example, you may decide that you will only take a risk of 2% of your funds on any single trade. If you have $100,000 in your trading account, and your stop loss (see below) is set at 5%, then this means that the maximum trade size you will employ is (($100,000×2%)/ 5) x 100 = $40,000. If your stop loss is triggered, you will lose $2,000.

Using this sort of risk management strategy means that you would have to have 50 losing trades in a row to see your account fall to zero. Position size management should go hand in hand with a disciplined stop loss philosophy.

Stop Loss Orders

Knowing your maximum downside, the most you are prepared to lose on a trade, is one of the main rules of risk management when trading stocks. Utilizing a stop loss order on each position you open will mean that your trading system and strategy removes the emotional tie to a trade, and helps to keep your trading disciplined. Losses will occur: capping those losses is a key to profitability.

When your position moves into being profitable, then you can use a stop loss to prevent profits evaporating. Many traders use a trailing stop to take advantage of increasing profits whilst limiting the downside at increasing prices.

Diversification and Hedging

My grandmother once told me I should never have all my eggs in one basket. It was until I started stock trading that I really understood what she meant.

It's easier to lose money if all your funds are in a single stock, than if you have spread across several. Some win, some lose. It's the way of the market. Even if you are trading in only one sector, then you should consider spreading your funds across several stocks.

Becoming good in different market sectors is even better: when one sector is cold, another will be hot. Diversifying isn't just about spreading risk, it's about creating opportunity.

Similarly, there are times when you will need to hedge your position. You may have a stock position with the results due. Taking an opposite position by way of options, for example, will mean that your position is protected over the time of the results. You can then unwind the hedge when trading has calmed down.

Some traders hedge their day trading book by taking a long position in one stock, and a short position in another 'look=alike' stock, hoping to profit on both.

Pick Your Spots

This will be part of your trading strategy. Pick the prices at which you are happy to buy and sell your stock. Use limit orders and other order types to maximize these opportunities.

You might use technical analysis and charts to provide directional decisions, or you might trade with a longer term view and employ fundamental analysis methodology. Whatever you choose, knowing your buying and selling levels will mean you trade with more conviction and with greater relaxation and discipline.

Your trading levels will also impact upon your stop loss orders, and your profit taking and exit strategy.

Cut your losses, Run Your Profits

Some traders have a target and take profits when that target is met. Others allow profitable positions to run, perhaps utilizing trailing stops to help maximize profits.

A good profitable trader will cut losses, maybe by using stop loss orders as described above.

It stands to reason that if you are disciplined, sticking to maximum loss levels and picking your spots for buying and selling, and then reacting accordingly, by cutting losses and running profits your trading results will benefit.

A gain isn't a gain until it has been realized

Remember that at some time you need to take your profits. It's not money until it's in your bank account. This means that you need to be aware of what profit you want to take from your trade. Too many traders see a position move to their target price, and then decide to hang on for a few more pennies: after all the stock is hot.

When the stock moves down a little, they continue to hang on: it's just a temporary downside in an upward trend. Then the unthinkable happens. The stock falls through the price at which they bought the stock.

Don't get caught in this trap. Risk management doesn't stop at knowing when to take a loss or how to minimize losses: it's also about knowing when to take profits.

The Bottom Line

Good trading isn't about always picking the right stocks, or the right prices. It's as much about managing your risk, and integrating a strong risk management philosophy into your trading strategy. A senior market maker once told me that a trader isn't a trader until he's lost $10,000 on a single transaction. Employing good risk management will mean this never happens to you.

Here are the tips that will help you improve your risk management instantly and avoid the most common problems that cause traders to lose money.

Setting orders and the reward: risk ratio

When you spot an entry signal, think where you'd place your stop loss and take profit order FIRST. Once you've identified reasonable price levels for your orders, measure the risk: reward ratio. If it doesn't match your requirements, skip the trade. Don't try to widen your take profit order or tighten your stop loss to achieve a higher reward: risk ratio.

The reward of a trade is always uncertain and potential. The risk is the only think you can control about your trade.

Most amateur traders do this the opposite way: they come up with a random reward: risk ratio and then manipulate their stop and profit orders to achieve their ratio.

Avoid break-even stops

Moving the stop loss to the point of the entry and so creating a "no risk" trade is a hazardous and often unprofitable maneuver. Whereas it's good and advisable to protect your position, the break-even strategy often leads to a variety of problems.

Especially if you are trading based on common technical analysis (support/resistance, chart patterns, highs and lows, or moving averages), your point of entry is usually very obvious and many traders will have a very similar entry. Of course, the pros know that and you can often see that price retraces back and squeezes the amateurs at the very obvious price levels, just before price then turns back into the original direction. A break-even stop will get out of potentially profitable trades if you move your stop too soon.

Never even use fixed stop distances

Many trading strategies tell you to use a fixed amount of points/pips on your stop loss and take profit orders across different instruments and even markets. Those "shortcuts" and generalizations completely neglect how price moves naturally and how financial markets work.

Volatility and momentum are constantly changing and, therefore, how much price moves in any given day and how much it fluctuates changes all the time. In times of higher volatility, you should set your stop loss and take profit orders wider to avoid premature stop runs and to maximize profits when price swings more. And in times of low volatility you have to set your orders closer to your entry and not be overly optimistic.

Secondly, trading with fixed distances doesn't let you chose reasonable price levels and it also takes away all the flexibility you need to have as a trader. Always be aware of important price levels and barriers such as round numbers, big moving averages, Fibonacci levels or just plain support and resistance.

Always compare win rate and reward: risk together

Many traders claim that the figure win rate is useless. But those traders miss a very important point. While observing the win rate alone will provide you with no valuable insights, combining win rate and risk: reward ratio can be seen as the Holy Grail in trading.

It's so important to understand that you either need an insanely high win rate, or have to ride your trades for a very long time. For example, a system with a win rate of 40% (which is what many professional traders average) only requires a reward: risk ratio of greater than 1.6 to trade profitably.

Trying to achieve an astronomical high win rate or believing that you have to ride trades for a long time often create wrong expectations and then leads to wrong assumptions and, finally, to mistakes in how traders approach their trading.

Don't use daily performance targets

Many traders will randomly set daily or weekly performance targets. Such an approach is very dangerous, and you have to stop thinking regarding daily or weekly returns. Setting yourself daily goals creates a lot of pressure and it usually also creates a "need to trade". Instead, here are some ideas on how to set trading goals the right way:

Short-term (daily and weekly): Focus on the best possible trade execution and on how well you follow your rules/plan.

Mid-term (weekly and monthly): Follow a professional routine, plan your trades in advance, obey your rules, journal your trades, review your trades and make sure that you learn the correct lessons.

Longer-term (semiannually): Review your trades, focusing on how well you executed your trades to get an understanding of your level of professionalism. Find weaknesses in your trading and adjust accordingly. This will lead to profitable trading inevitably.

Position sizing like a pro

When it comes to position sizing, traders usually pick a random number such as 1%, 2% or 3%, and then apply it to all their trades without ever thinking about position sizing again.

Trading is an activity of chance, such as professional betting or poker. In those activities, it's common practice to vary the amount you wager, based on the likelihood of the outcome. If you hold a very strong hand in poker, you'd bet more than when you see almost no chances of winning, right?

The same holds true for trading. If you trade multiple setups or strategies, you will see that each setup and strategy has a different win rate and also that the reward: risk ratios on different strategies vary. Thus, you should reduce your position size on setups with a lower win rate and increase the position size when your win rate is higher.

Following the approach of dynamic position sizing will help you reduce your account volatility and potentially help you improve account growth.

Using the reward: risk ratio and R-multiple together

Whereas the reward: risk ratio is more of a potential metric where you measure the distances to your stop and profit target when you enter the trade, the R-multiple is a performance measurement, and it describes the outcome of your trades.

When entering trades, traders are often too optimistic and set profit targets too far or close their profitable trades too early which will then decrease their initial reward: risk ratio. By analyzing how your R-multiple compares to your reward: risk ratio, you can get new insights into your trading. If you see major deviations, you should look deeper and try to find what it causing the differences.

Take spread seriously

For the most liquid instruments, spreads are usually just a few pips and, therefore, traders view them as they weren't even existent.

Research shows that only about 1% of all day traders are able to profit net of fees.

The average day trader usually holds his trades for anywhere between 5 and 200 pips. If the spread on your instrument is 2 pips, this will mean that you pay a fee of 10% on trades with a profit of 20 pips. And even if you hold your trade for 50 pips, the spread amounts to almost 5%. Those costs can result in significant drawbacks for your trading system and even turn a winning into a losing system. Therefore, start monitoring spread closely and avoid instruments or times where spreads are high.

Correlations – increasing risk unknowingly

If you are a forex trader, you can often see a very strong correlation between certain forex pairs. If you are a stock trader, you will notice that companies within the same industries and sectors, or which are based in the same country, often move together over long periods.

When it comes to money- and risk management this means that trading instruments which are positively correlated lead to increased risk. Let's illustrate this with an example:

Let's say you bought the EUR/USD and the GBP/USD, and you are risked 1.5% on each trade; the correlation between those 2 instruments is highly positive (close to +0.90). This means that if the EUR/USD goes up 1%, the GBP/USD goes up 0.90% as well. Having a long position in both the EUR/USD and the GBP/USD is then equal to having 1 position open and risking 2.7% on it [(1.5%+1.5%)*0.9=2.7%].

Of course, this is a very simplistic way of looking at correlations, but it gives you an idea of what to keep in mind when trading correlated instruments.

Top trading stock secret

There is an overwhelming amount of financial advisors in the world today. There are many people who benefit from a financial advisor but for the majority of us, a financial advisor is not needed. Most brokerage firms do not want to help you if you have less than $100,000 to invest. Here I will outline two secrets to get beginners trading stock on their own without a financial advisor.

Tip 1: Open a brokerage account. The first step to trading stock is opening a discount brokerage account. A discount brokerage account allows you access to purchase or sell stocks without an advisor. These accounts are different than traditional brokerage accounts as they are charge lesser fees and you do not receive any advice. You really do not need the advice, most times the advice you would receive from an advisor is information already accessible to you. They do not always have the inside scoop and if they did have the inside scoop they could not tell you. Giving a client information that is not already public is call insider trading and it is a felony. The information the advisor provides could be found by you saving you unnecessary fees. Once you open the account it is time to start trading.

Tip 2: Tailor your investment plan to your personality. There is no "one" way to investing in stocks. Once you learn and understand the basics you can make your portfolio represent who you are as a person. You cannot do everything the television commentator says. If you are interested in retail stores it would not make sense to invest in banks because some hot shot billionaire says this is where you should invest.

These are the two secrets to beginners trading stocks. I would also add to make sure you are comfortable with your trades. It does not make sense if you cannot sleep at night because of your choice in stocks. Your first objective is to avoid major losses. If you protect your capital, you can always find ways to make money.

Chapter 5

PROS and CONS OF SIMPLE DAY TRADING STOCKS.

Pros

Risking personal money for a potential gain is a big step for some individuals. Investors willing to take the risk often use their finances to invest in the stock market. A stock market is an exchange place where investors meet to buy and sell shares. Historically, the stock market has experienced positive returns over the long run, but there are advantages and disadvantages of investing in the stock market.

Return on Investment

Historical returns related to stock market investing outperform many other types of investments. According to Vanguard, the historical average return for stocks from 1926 to 2011 is 9.9 percent. In contrast, the average return for bonds during the same period is 5.6 percent. Placing your finances in the stock market gives you the opportunity to grow your finances over the long-term. Many well-established companies also pay dividends to investors, which increases your overall return on investment.

Ownership

Investing in the stock market is one of the easiest ways to become a minority owner within a company. When you buy shares of a company's stock, you take an ownership stake in the business. Although the ownership percentage is relatively small, you receive

59

the right to vote on certain business decisions and corporate leadership. Unlike some other types of businesses, you can easily exit out of your ownership stake by simply selling the shares to someone else desiring to invest in the stock market.

You're 100% Cash at the Beginning and End of Every Day!

What a feeling! It's easy to sleep well at night when you're in 100% cash. Even though this is often touted as a good reason to day trade, you still won't appreciate it until you experience it. Imagine waking up in the morning and something comes up that will keep you away from the markets that day (sickness, errands, whatever). If you're swing trading, being away from the markets will take its toll – it will always be in the back of your mind. If you're day trading, you're sitting in cash so just take a day off.

You'll Have Twice as Much Buying Power

Once you refine your system, this is a big benefit. You'll be able to trade more opportunities because you'll have 4 times your account equity in intraday buying power. This startles a lot of newcomers, but if you have a handle on your risk this leverage is very valuable.

You Actually Earn Interest on your Overnight Cash Balance

This one was very surprising to me. One of the reasons most non-day traders shy away from using margin is because you actually have to PAY interest when you use it. Most brokers leave your cash account in an interest bearing account, so when you have cash in it you'll actually be making money. Here's the important point: interest is paid on the overnight cash balance, so because you're 100% cash you'll be earning interest just as if you had your money in a savings account. Last I checked my Cyber Trader account earned 5% interest or so. This is like earning the better part of 1R each month for doing nothing.

You'll gather a Statistically Meaningful Sample Size Far More Quickly

Because you'll have more opportunities to trade, you'll gather a much larger sample size much more quickly. This is vitally important for good trading. Let's say you make 30 trades in a month. That's a decent sample size to begin delving into and to start learning from. If you're trading on a longer time frame, it could take you much longer to make 30 trades so it will take far longer to learn how your system really works.

You Can Completely Ignore the News

The vast majority of price affecting news like earnings reports is released after market hours. You don't have to worry about holding overnight when a company is releasing earnings or when, let's say, the FBI raids a company's headquarters (d'oh!). You don't need to worry about how you're going to react to the news – you can just let other people worry about the news and trade their reactions.

Day Trading Can Actually Be Less Risky

Because you'll be avoiding those overnight gaps, with proper money management you can really have better control of your risk. Losses of greater than 2R are fairly common when holding overnight, but they are quite rare when day trading.

Cons.

Subject to Higher Risk

When investing in the stock market, the higher the return, the greater the risk of losing money. Stock market prices are linked to the issuing company's earnings. When a company is experiencing financial difficulties, the price of the stock can decline rapidly. Stock market volatility can lead to a substantial loss of investment. If the majority of the market is experiencing loss and leaving the market because of economic factors, you may find it difficult to sell your shares to someone else.

The key corresponding disadvantage of stock market trading, one wrong move can cost your entire capital amount and beyond, depending on whether or not your positions are leveraged. Managing risk as one of the key threats to your trading is an essential component of any effective trading strategy, and understanding from the off that markets can move heavily against you in the blink of an eye is crucial to success.

Time Consuming

Investing in the stock market is not like playing the lottery. You need to perform research and investment analysis to find potentially profitable stock. For many individuals, investing in the stock market is a time-consuming, complex task. Even after you find a stock to buy, you must monitor the movement of the stock's price. Although many investors implement a long-term buy and hold strategy, it is important to know when to exit a stock position if it turns out to be a bad investment choice. Investment in NSE is not as easy as investing in a lottery as you have to complete many formalities in the process and hence is time consuming.

Stock market trading is wildly popular across the globe, with billions traded in company securities and assets across many millions of investors. For the businesses selling their securities, stock market trading provides a key mechanism for raising finance, while also giving life to pensions, savings funds and individual investment portfolios. But like any activity, stock market trading has both advantages and disadvantages that must be weighed up in determining whether it's a worthwhile pursuit for the individual would-be investor.

Trading Advantages

Rate of Return

Perhaps the main advantage stock market trading brings to the table is its inherent ability to deliver significant rates of returns. Contrasted with an interest-bearing bank account which might pay 5% per annum if you're lucky (without factoring in applicable taxes and the impact of inflation on the value of capital), stock market trading can see a 5% return over the course of one day, and oftentimes even more for the shrewd investor.

Acquisition of Assets

Unlike speculating on index movements, trading on the stock markets sees the acquisition of real, valuable assets in the form of the shares that are bought. Unless something goes disastrously wrong with the underlying business, any shares you acquire will retain some value that can be extracted at a later stage, making it a more secure investment with life-long value locked in.

Dividend Yield

Because shares entitle the bearer to an annual dividend payment on a per share basis, they also produce an ongoing revenue stream in the good times. Furthermore, the payment of dividends receives a more favourable tax treatment in the UK, with basic-rate tax paying recipients in effect paying 0% on the dividend revenue they receive.

Knowledge

When you're trading the markets, you're effectively competing with the know-how, resources and intuition of professional traders and real experts. It is critical therefore that you develop the knowledge necessary to execute effective trades and interpret the way in which the markets are likely to move, which requires hard work, effort and a great deal of trial and error when you first start out.

Unpredictability

Markets aren't always easy to read, and even the most experienced traders can get it horribly wrong. By their very nature markets are unpredictable, and can completely turn in an instant – otherwise, every single trader would be a multi-millionaire.

Volatile Investments

Investment in BSE is subjected to many risks since the market is volatile. The shares of a company go up and come down so many times in just a single day. These price fluctuations are unpredictable most of the times, and the investor sometimes has to face severe loss due to such uncertainty.

Brokerage Commissions Kill Profit Margin

Every time an investor buys or sells his shares, he has to pay some amount as a brokerage commission to the broker, which kills the profit margin.

Manufactured by Amazon.ca
Bolton, ON

18211046R00039